Guide Dogs

by Jessica Rudolph

Consultant: Kathy Zubrycki
Director of Training and Admissions
Guiding Eyes for the Blind, Inc.
Yorktown Heights, New York

BEARPORT
PUBLISHING

New York, New York

Credits
Cover and Title Page, © altrendo images/Altrendo/Getty; 4, © iStockphoto/Thinkstock; 4–5, © Associated Press; 6–7, © Koen Suyk/ANP/Newscom; 8–9, © Robin Nelson/Zuma Press/Corbis; 10–11, © Keystone Pressedienst/Zuma Press/Newscom; 12–13, © Pablo Vazquez Digital Press Photos/Newscom; 14–15, © Markus Altmann/Corbis; 16, © William Mullins/Alamy; 16–17, © Kathy deWitt/Alamy; 18–19, © Amanda Voisard/Zuma Press/Newscom; 18, © Zuma Press/Alamy; 20–21, © Pei Xin Xinhua News Agency/Newscom; 22, © Victoria Yee; 23TL, © Amanda Voisard/Zuma Press/Newscom; 23TR, © Lars Christensen/Shutterstock; 23BL, © F1online digitale Bildagentur GmbH/Alamy; 23BR, © altrendo images.

Publisher: Kenn Goin
Creative Director: Spencer Brinker
Design: Debrah Kaiser
Photo Researcher: Michael Win

Library of Congress Cataloging-in-Publication Data

Rudolph, Jessica.
  Guide dogs / by Jessica Rudolph.
      pages cm. — (Bow-WOW! dog helpers series)
  Includes bibliographical references and index.
  Audience: Age 5–8.
  ISBN 978-1-62724-118-2 (library binding) — ISBN 1-62724-118-3 (library binding)
  1. Guide dogs—Juvenile literature. I. Title.
  HV1780.R83 2014
  362.4'183—dc23
                                                2013032376

For more information, write to Bearport Publishing Company, Inc., 45 West 21st Street, Suite 3B, New York, New York 10010. Printed in the United States of America.

10 9 8 7 6 5 4 3 2 1

Contents

Meet a Guide Dog

I'm a **guide dog**.

My owner, Jake, is blind.

Arf!

4

5

Guide dogs like me have a special job.

We help our owners get around safely.

A guide dog's owner is called a **handler**.

6

A guide dog wears a **harness**.

The handler holds on to it.

The handler tells the dog where to go.

Guide dogs lead their handlers to stores and other places.

harness

9

Roads are dangerous places.

Guide dogs stop at street corners.

Then our owners know to stop, too.

Blind people need to be careful when they cross streets. They cannot see cars zoom by.

At street corners, handlers listen carefully.

They wait for the sounds of cars to stop.

Then they say the **command** "Forward."

When a guide dog hears "Forward," it leads its handler across the street.

Blind people can fall going up or down stairs.

A guide dog stops in front of stairs.

Then the handler knows to carefully take the next step.

A guide dog stops when any kind of danger is in front of its handler.

How do dogs learn to guide blind people?

As puppies, we go to school!

GUIDE DOG PUPPY

Guide dogs have to be very smart and friendly.

Guide dog puppy in training

At school, pups are taught many commands.

We learn to sit.

We also learn to stay calm around loud traffic.

When a guide dog finishes school, it goes to live with its new handler.

Guide dogs keep their handlers safe.

Handlers give their dogs food, water, and lots of love.

Together, they make a great team!

After working, guide dogs rest or play with their owners.

Guide Dog Facts

- Many kinds of dogs become guide dogs. Most are German shepherds, golden retrievers, or Labrador retrievers.

- Guide dog training takes about six months.

- Do not pet a guide dog without first asking its handler for permission.

Glossary

command (kuh-MAND)
an order given by a
person to do something

guide dog (GIDE DAWG)
a dog that is trained to
lead a person who is blind
from place to place

handler (HAND-lur)
a person who takes care
of and lives with a guide
dog

harness (HAR-niss)
a strap with a handle
worn by a guide dog that
its handler holds on to

Index

Read More

McGinty, Alice B. *Guide Dogs: Seeing for People Who Can't (Dogs Helping People).* New York: PowerKids Press (1999).

Richter, Abigail. *Guide Dogs (Rosen Real Readers).* New York: Rosen (2002).

Learn More Online

To learn more about guide dogs, visit
www.bearportpublishing.com/Bow-WOW!

About the Author

Jessica Rudolph lives in Connecticut. She has edited and written many books about history, science, and nature for children.